Strength That Rises From Within

FINDING LIGHT IN THE FIGHT

...

A JOURNEY OF FAITH, COURAGE, AND RESILIENCE

MARILYN SPEIGHTS

ISBN: 979-8-218-77942-9

Published by HMSM Publishing

Cover Design by Be Celebrated Printing

Printed in the United States of America

ACKNOWLEDGMENTS

First and foremost, I want to express my deepest gratitude to **God**, my ultimate source of strength and healing. Your presence in my life, especially during the darkest days, has been the foundation of my journey. Without you, none of this would have been possible.

To my wonderful husband, **Howard**, thank you for being my rock, my partner, and my constant source of love and encouragement. You have been there every step of the way. Your unwavering support gave me the courage to keep fighting. I am forever grateful for you! You never let me lose hope, and your constant encouragement gave me the courage to write this book and share my truth. Your belief in this project and in me helped make this book a reality.

To my amazing children, **Shatay and Markell**, thank you for your love and patience. You are my greatest treasures, and you made it all worth it. You gave me a reason to fight and reminded me each day what joy and resilience look like. Watching you grow through this with grace and compassion made me even more determined to heal. You are my true motivation.

A special thank you to my daughter, **Shatay**, who not only walked through this in her youth, but also served as the editor of this book. Your careful eye, thoughtful feedback, and heartfelt support helped bring these words to life. I'm so proud of the woman you are.

A heartfelt thanks goes to my **family**: my parents, siblings, and extended family. Your love and support, whether near or far, kept me going. Your prayers, meals, check-ins, and presence made all the difference. I felt your love surround me, and I didn't feel alone. Your support helped carry me through. You are my foundation, and I appreciate you more than words can express.

To my **church family**, thank you for your unwavering prayers, love, and support. Your faith has been an anchor for me. A special thank you goes to my senior pastors for spiritual covering, every prayer lifted, word spoken, and moment of care you showed. You both reminded me that the church is not just a building; it is a family that rallies around one another. You were there to lift me up spiritually when I needed it most. Additionally, I'd be remised if I didn't mention the incredible women in my church family who have also overcome breast cancer. I honor your courage, resilience, and trust in God. You are living reminders that God still heals, strengthens, and sustains. Your testimonies of perseverance have inspired me. You remind me, and all of us, that no one is ever alone in the fight. May this book reflect the same light of hope that shines through each of you.

To my **medical team**, who walked this journey with me, thank you for your expertise and care. To my oncologists, surgeons, and nurses, your compassion, knowledge, and care were answered prayers. You guided me through the treatments, the recovery, and the countless unknowns with wisdom and kindness. I am so grateful for each and every one of you.

Thank you to the **survivors and support groups** I had the privilege of connecting with. Your stories, wisdom, and strength were a lifeline for me during some of my toughest times. You showed me that I was never alone in this fight.

Finally, I want to acknowledge **every woman** who has fought or is currently battling with breast cancer. This book is dedicated to you and your strength. You are my inspiration, and I hope my story offers you hope and encouragement in your own journey. May you find hope in these pages, and may you always know you are not alone.

FOREWORD

The first time I heard my wife's breast cancer diagnosis felt like a burning dagger piercing through every ounce of my being. In an instant, our entire life dynamic had changed. In that moment, I felt like life had dealt us a disservice. However, after the tears and comforting embraces, we gathered our emotions to the best of our ability, considering what we had just learned. At that point, we knew we had to rely on our faith. We were no longer just husband and wife. We had to become prayer warriors, caregivers, and fighters in a battle we never asked for but were determined to face together and WIN.

To witness how Marilyn took this fight head on with this beast of a disease speaks to her enormous faith and passion for life. This journey was both heartbreaking and inspiring. I saw her rise with courage, even on the days when she had every reason to give up. I saw her choose faith over fear, hope over despair, and strength over surrender. Seeing how she embraced the sovereignty of God's power, I witnessed not just the fight for her health, but also the fight to stay whole in mind, body, and spirit.

This book is her story, but it's also our story. It's a story of pain, yes, but also a story that we chose to make together, as we moved in the power of God. It's a testament to the grace of God, the resilience of a strong woman, and the quiet strength that love provides in the darkest of times.

To every person reading these pages, whether you're battling cancer, supporting someone who is, or simply searching for hope, I pray you find encouragement here. I know firsthand the depth of my wife's faith and the heart behind her words. What you hold in your hands is not just a book but evidence that even in the face of life's hardest storms, you can come out stronger, better, and not bitter.

I am grateful for the opportunity to experience this journey alongside Marilyn and am so proud of her for sharing her story and testimony with the world.

Honored to walk this journey with you.

Your loving husband,
Howard

TABLE OF CONTENTS

INTRODUCTION

. . .

A JOURNEY BEGINS

I was 37 years old and married to the love of my life, with two young children: one just 3 years old, the other 7. Life felt like it was unfolding just as it should. We were in the prime of our lives, filled with excitement and dreams for the future. I was thriving in my career with a job I loved working outside the home. My husband and I had recently purchased our first house, a place we could call our own and fill with love and laughter.

We were building a life that was everything we had ever dreamed of. We were healthy, our family was strong, and our days were filled with the vibrant energy of young children.

We had the kind of life most people aspire to, filled with love, laughter, and the joy of watching our children grow. There was always something to do, somewhere to go, and memories to be made. We even found time to travel, exploring new places and creating cherished moments together as a family. It felt like we had it all. Everything was in perfect alignment. I was living a life I loved, one I believed would continue on this upward trajectory.

But life, as we all know, throws curveballs when we least expect them. During a routine self-breast exam in the shower, I first noticed a small, hard lump. It was about the size of a pea, just near my breast chest line. I remember thinking it was probably nothing, maybe just a change in my body that would pass with time. However, after a few months, it did not go away, and I could no longer ignore it. So, I decided to get it checked out, not thinking for a second that it would be anything serious.

The day I went to the doctor was a day that would forever be etched in my memory. It was the same morning the world was shaken by the news of the airplanes flying into the Twin Towers. The tragedy that was unfolding in the world hit like a shockwave, and amid all that chaos, I was about to face a storm of my own. My doctor felt the lump and immediately decided to perform an ultrasound to further investigate the abnormal finding. The lump, or abnormal tissue, was detected during the physical exam, so the ultrasound could help provide more information. It can distinguish between solid masses (which may be benign or cancerous) and fluid-filled cysts (which are usually benign).

The ultrasound showed something suspicious, and I was quickly referred to a surgeon for a biopsy. A breast biopsy is a medical procedure used to remove a small sample of tissue from a suspicious area in the breast for testing and analysis. This was to determine whether a lump or abnormality in the breast was cancerous or benign (non-cancerous). It is an important diagnostic tool that helps doctors make an accurate diagnosis when there are concerns about a possible breast cancer diagnosis. At that moment, the reality of the situation began to sink in. I knew something wasn't right, but I was still trying to hold onto hope, convincing myself that I was too young for this to be anything serious. After all, I was just 37, and breast cancer seemed like something that affected older women. I kept telling myself it couldn't be what I feared, that it was just a benign issue that would soon resolve itself.

But then, the phone call that would change my life forever finally came. I was blindsided. When I received the news that the small lump was, in fact, a cancerous tumor, I was in complete shock. It felt surreal. No one in my family had ever gone through anything like this. I could hardly process the words the doctor was saying. A feeling of deep, sudden devastation washed over me, compounded by the chaos unfolding in the world around me. Everything I had taken for granted about my life suddenly felt so fragile and uncertain.

That day marked the beginning of a journey I never could have anticipated, a journey that would challenge me in ways I hadn't prepared for. However, as I stand here today, I realize that this book is not just about my fight with breast cancer. It is about hope, resilience, and healing. Through this journey, I discovered strength I never knew I had, and I found peace and faith in places I hadn't expected.

This story is for anyone who may find themselves facing an unexpected storm, whether it's cancer or any other challenge. I want to offer a message of encouragement, an invitation to press on, even when the road ahead seems impossible. I want to share the hope I found, the strength I discovered, and the healing I experienced along the way.

This is my story, yes, but it's also a message to others who may be walking this path: there is always hope.

THE STRENGTH THAT RISES FROM WITHIN

Even in the darkest moments, when it feels like all is lost, there is a glimmer of light. Through that light, we can find the courage to keep going, the strength to heal, and the resilience to overcome.

1

• • •

THE DIAGNOSIS: THE GROUND SHIFT

The moment I heard the word "cancerous," it felt like the ground beneath me shifted. One moment, I was living a life I loved, full of joy, energy, and dreams for the future. The next, I was confronted with a reality that felt almost impossible to accept. I had worked so hard to stay calm when I first discovered that small, hard lump in my breast. I told myself it was probably nothing, just a harmless change. But as the days turned into weeks, and the lump didn't go away, I couldn't ignore it any longer.

THE STRENGTH THAT RISES FROM WITHIN

The ultrasound and biopsy came swiftly, within a week's time. Waiting for the results felt like an eternity. Each passing day seemed to stretch on forever as I prepared myself for whatever news was coming.

When the call finally came with the results, I felt like the wind had been knocked out of me. The words that followed hit me like a freight train: **Ductal Carcinoma in Situ**. It was breast cancer but not in the form I had expected. It was localized and contained within the ducts, meaning it hadn't spread. But it was still cancerous, nonetheless. The big C! The words echoed in my mind, reverberating through every cell of my being. It was as if the whole world had suddenly gone still. I felt crushed under the weight of it. I was disappointed, overwhelmed, and completely uncertain of what was to come. *How could this be happening to me? Why wasn't I immune?*

I remember standing there in the doctor's office, looking at the medical report and being unable to fully process the words on the page in front of me. My mind raced as I thought of my family, my children, who were so young and so full of life. *How could I possibly go through something like this?* No one in my family had ever experienced anything like this before. Cancer was a disease I associated with older women, not someone like me. I had so much life still to live.

At that moment, everything seemed to crumble. I couldn't make sense of it. The life I had been living, one of health, joy, and anticipation, suddenly felt so fragile and easily threatened. The dream of what my life was supposed to be seemed to dissolve in the blink of an eye. I wanted to wake up from this nightmare. I wanted the tumor to vanish, the diagnosis to be reversed, and to somehow be healed instantly and without struggle. But deep down, I knew that wasn't how life worked.

I knew that this journey was about to change everything, in ways I couldn't yet fathom.

The days after the diagnosis were a blur. A whirlwind of emotions took over me: fear, doubt, sadness, and even anger. The future, once full of promise, suddenly seemed so uncertain, like walking through fog. I kept asking myself: *How do I fight something I can't even see? How do I face something so big, so scary, so unknown?*

And yet, in the quiet moments, after the emotional storm had passed, I began to pray. Prayer became my lifeline. I prayed for strength, for clarity, for healing, for courage. I wasn't sure what the next steps would look like, but I knew I had to keep moving forward. I had to gather whatever strength I had left to fight, not just for myself, but for my children, for my husband, and for the life I wanted to continue living.

Amid all the fear and uncertainty, there came a moment of clarity. It was the hardest decision I would ever have to make: to choose hope over fear. To stop dwelling on the "what ifs" and start focusing on the "what now." I chose to fight. I decided that cancer would not define me. It would not steal my joy, my hope, or my future.

The road ahead would not be easy, and I knew there would be times of doubt, pain, and exhaustion. But I also knew this: I had the strength within me to keep moving forward, no matter what. And so, the journey began. One step at a time, I chose hope; I chose faith; and I chose life.

2

. . .

THE PHYSICAL REALITY:
NAVIGATING TREATMENT

The day I learned I had cancer was the beginning of a journey into the unknown. As I moved through the treatment process, I quickly discovered just how much my body would be tested, not only by the cancer but also by the treatments designed to save me.

I had **breast-conserving surgery**, also known as a **lumpectomy**, along with an **axillary lymph node dissection**, which was supposed to remove the cancer and prevent it from spreading.

Breast-conserving surgery is a treatment option that aims to remove the tumor while preserving as much of the breast tissue as possible. During this procedure, only the part of the breast that has cancer was removed. The remainder of the breast is left intact. The cancerous lump, or abnormal tissue, along with a small margin of normal breast tissue around it, is removed to ensure no microscopic cancer cells remain in the area.

In addition to the breast tissue, doctors may also remove some of the lymph nodes under the arm to determine if the cancer has spread there. Breast cancer often spreads to these lymph nodes, which act as filters for the body's lymphatic system. If the cancer has spread to the lymph nodes, it can then spread to other parts of the body, a process called **metastasizing**. For me, the doctors performed an axillary lymph node dissection to remove several lymph nodes and check for signs of cancer. Fortunately, thank God, the surgery was successful and my lymph nodes were clear. This was such a relief. The cancer had not spread to this area, and it was still contained within the breast. This was a key moment of hope in my journey, but I knew I still had a long road ahead.

Radiation Therapy: Targeting Cancer Cells Post-Surgery

Ensuring that the cancer didn't return, I underwent **35 rounds of radiation therapy** over seven weeks. Daily trips to the radiation center became routine, but the fatigue, skin irritation, and emotional toll were not so easily managed.

Radiation therapy became a pivotal part of my healing process. After the surgery, even though the cancerous tumor had been removed, there was a need to ensure that any lingering cancer cells were eradicated from my body. Radiation would be the final step in making sure the cancer didn't return.

Radiation uses high-energy rays, often X-rays, directed at the breast tissue to destroy any remaining cancer cells. In my case, radiation was targeted to the area where the tumor had been, as well as surrounding tissue, to prevent any potential microscopic cancer cells from growing again.

The treatment itself was quick and painless, but the aftermath was something I didn't anticipate. I had daily sessions that lasted about five to ten minutes. Including setting up machinery, they could last up to 20 minutes. I had to lie still while the radiation beams were precisely aimed at my breast, ensuring that the surrounding healthy tissue was spared. Though seeming easy at first, as the days went on, I began to feel the effects on my skin. The area treated with radiation became red, burned, and felt tender to the touch, almost like a bad sunburn. Not soon after these treatments began, we went on a family trip to Disney World in Florida for the kids' spring break. I didn't want to disappoint my children or get in the way of their fun. However, making matters worse, the heat from being in the sun all day made the treated area of my skin blistered and raw. In constant discomfort, it was hard not to feel like my body was being put through even more trauma. I had to remind myself that this was the final fight, the last step to being cancer-free.

The Fight Isn't Over: The Return of Cancer

Just as I thought I was beginning to put the worst behind me, the unthinkable happened.

As I was approaching my 5th anniversary of being cancer-free, the cancer came back. This time, it was **Triple Negative Breast Cancer** in the same breast. This type of breast cancer is a serious case that requires aggressive treatment like chemotherapy to kill rapidly growing cancer cells. Because it doesn't have the usual receptors and is harder to treat, it tends to grow and spread faster than other types of breast cancer. It's most common with younger women and especially so with Black and Hispanic women. I was devastated. I had already fought so hard, and the thought of going through everything all over again was almost too much to bear. But I had no choice. I chose to fight again.

This time, the treatment plan was even more aggressive. I had a **skin-sparing mastectomy**, a type of breast surgery performed to treat breast cancer while preserving as much of the breast tissue as possible. During this procedure, the surgeon removed my breast tissue, including the tumor and any affected areas, leaving the skin of the breast intact. The goal was to remove the cancerous tissue while maintaining the natural shape of the breast's skin, which was beneficial for my reconstructive surgery after the mastectomy, providing both medical and emotional benefits.

The surgery itself was a success, but the doctors told me that I couldn't undergo reconstruction surgery until they knew for sure that all my margins were clear. The uncertainty hung over me. However, just days after the surgery, I received the good news: all the margins were clear and negative, and I could go forward with the reconstruction process. But after everything I'd been through, I chose to wait. I couldn't bring myself to go through another surgery so soon.

So, for a couple of years, I wore a prosthesis. The **breast prosthesis** is a specially designed artificial breast that can be worn to restore the appearance of the breast after a mastectomy (the surgical removal of one or both breasts). It was worn inside my bra and was made to resemble the natural shape and feel of a real breast. It was an important option for me since I chose not to undergo immediate breast reconstruction and a temporary solution while waiting for reconstruction to be performed. It wasn't perfect, but it was enough to help me navigate life in a way that felt somewhat normal.

Chemotherapy: A Brutal but Necessary Battle

Chemotherapy, however, was a whole different experience. Unbeknownst to me, I was about to face a treatment that would take me to my lowest physical and emotional points. I underwent five months of chemotherapy after my mastectomy to destroy any remaining cancer cells that might have been lurking elsewhere in my body. It wasn't just about fighting the cancer in my breast anymore; it was about preventing the cancer from spreading to other organs.

The chemo regimen was intense. I was on a combination of powerful chemotherapy drugs that were effective but hard on my body. The drugs were administered through an IV, and each round of treatment was scheduled every three weeks. I remember sitting in the chemo chair, hooked up to the infusion, and mentally preparing for the toll it would take on me. The first few rounds of chemotherapy were manageable, physically draining but bearable. Chemotherapy doesn't discriminate; it attacks rapidly dividing cells, both cancerous and healthy. This is why side effects can be so brutal. I lost my hair quickly, and not just from my head. Eyebrows, eyelashes, and body hair all disappeared in a matter of weeks. This loss, though a small thing in the grand scheme of cancer treatment, was another blow to my sense of self.

The fatigue was overwhelming. I couldn't escape it. My body felt as if it had been drained of all energy, and the simplest tasks became insurmountable. The third day after each round of chemo was the hardest. I could barely get out of bed and struggled to even eat or drink. Though mostly controllable, the nausea was constant, and the metallic taste in my mouth made eating difficult. Even the thought of food was enough to make me feel queasy.

Beyond the physical exhaustion, the emotional toll was just as challenging. I found myself questioning how much more I could take. I questioned how my body would respond and if it would ever return to its normal state. At times, I wanted to give up. But something inside me told me I had to keep going. I would cry in my husband's arms, not knowing what the next day would bring. Upon drying my tears and on each day that passed, I held on to the hope that this suffering would lead me to healing.

The Side Effects: A Constant Reminder of the Battle

The surgery, radiation, and chemotherapy treatments were successful, but the physical aftermath was far more than I had anticipated.

While the treatments worked to rid my body of cancer, the side effects were persistent, some of them catching me off guard. A few months after the treatments ended, I developed lymphedema in my arm, a condition I hadn't expected. Lymphedema is the swelling of tissue caused by a build-up of protein-rich fluid that would normally be drained through the lymphatic system. In my case, the removal of lymph nodes during surgery had disrupted the system, causing fluid to accumulate in my arm.

This condition didn't just affect my arm physically; it affected how I was able to maneuver day-to-day. The swelling limited the movement of my arm, making everyday tasks such as cooking, driving, or carrying groceries more difficult. It was as if my body was reminding me of the trauma it had been through, even though the cancer was gone. There was constant discomfort, and I became increasingly aware of how fragile my body felt. It was like I was always walking a fine line between healing and new challenges.

In addition to the physical discomfort, lymphedema carries serious risks. For example, it increases the chances of skin infections like cellulitis. I had to take extra care of my skin, as any small cut or bruise could become a major problem. The treatments for lymphedema were ongoing and multifaceted: compression bandages, manual lymphatic drainage massage, compression stockings, sequential pneumatic pumping, and a meticulous skincare routine became my new reality. Each of these treatments required time, patience, and attention. The swelling, though it would decrease somewhat over time, remained a constant reminder of everything my body had endured.

Even today, I continue to monitor my arm carefully, always aware of the potential for swelling and the complications that might arise. There are days when I still feel a twinge of discomfort and am reminded that the healing process is not linear. It's ongoing and not always easy. I've learned to live with my new normal, accepting that my body has gone through many changes. Nevertheless, this is still my body, and I'll do all I can to take care of it. I've also learned that it's okay to acknowledge the fragility of life. Lymphedema, while a constant challenge, has taught me to be more mindful, more patient, and more grateful for the days I feel strong and healthy. The swelling and discomfort may never fully go away, but I refuse to let it define me. Each day I manage it is a victory and proof that while my body has been through a battle, I continue to rise above the challenges, carrying on with strength, determination, and the knowledge that healing comes in many forms.

Reconstruction: Another Hurdle

Soon, after all I had gone through up to this point, I wanted my body back. I wanted to move past this chapter in my life, to reclaim something that felt like "me" again.

THE STRENGTH THAT RISES FROM WITHIN

Just when I thought I'd reached the end of the hardest part of my journey, there was another unexpected twist. While preparing for my breast reconstruction surgery prep testing, the doctors discovered a spot on my lung. The cancer had spreaded to this area. What was supposed to be routine testing turned into yet another major battle.

The doctors performed a **lung metastasectomy**, where a section of my lung was removed. This unexpected circumstance was both frightening and overwhelming. It was a reminder of how quickly life can change and how vital it is to hold on to faith. Waking up from that surgery, I felt both weak and grateful: the former because my body had endured so much, and the latter because, even in this, God had given me another chance at life.

This chapter of my journey reminded me that healing doesn't always follow the path we expect. Yet, through every scar, every delay, and every surprise diagnosis, I saw God's hand holding me steady. What the enemy meant for harm, God continued to use as part of my testimony. It was another reminder that my journey was largely about trusting God with every unexpected turn.

In 2012, I finally found the courage to go back for a **TRAM Flap** surgery. It was a big decision, one that required a lot of thought, but I wanted to regain control of my appearance and feel whole again. The surgery went well, and when I saw the results, I was overjoyed. For the first time in years, I felt like my body was truly my own again. The scars, though reminders of my journey, no longer felt like something I had to hide. I loved the results, and it felt like I had reclaimed something essential to my femininity.

The next year, I decided to have a breast reduction on the opposite breast so that everything would be symmetrical. It seemed like the final step in my physical recovery. But after the tissue from the opposite breast was removed, the doctors found cancer cells, **DCIS (Ductal Carcinoma in Situ)**, lurking in the tissue. Ductal Carcinoma in Situ is a non-invasive form of breast cancer. It was confined to the ducts in the breast and had not spread to other parts of the breast tissue or beyond. DCIS is considered an early form of breast cancer and is often diagnosed during routine screening mammograms, before it causes any symptoms.

I was shaken, but I had no choice but to keep moving forward. The cancer had returned in a new form, but, this time, I chose to have a total mastectomy with immediate **LD Flap reconstruction**. It was another intense surgery, but I was determined to put this behind me once and for all. The good news was that I wouldn't need any additional treatments. No more radiation. No more chemotherapy.

Instead, I would take maintenance medication every day for five years, which extended to 9 years, still a small price to pay to continue living cancer-free. Along with ongoing biannual doctor visits and various tests, I had a new routine to follow.

3

. . .

MENTAL AND EMOTIONAL HEALTH: FINDING STRENGTH

By now, I was tired. So tired. After everything I had been through (the surgeries, the treatments, the endless rounds of tests, the fear or hope of what each new day might bring, and the constant uncertainty) it felt like my body and spirit were running on empty. There were times when the weight of the fight seemed too heavy to bear and the thought of pushing forward felt impossible. All I had been through emotionally and physically had taken its toll, and I found myself questioning how much longer I could keep going.

THE STRENGTH THAT RISES FROM WITHIN

It was as if my very essence was stretched thin, and I wondered if I had the strength to go on.

But then, I would look at my husband, Howard, and my children, Shatay and Markell. Their faces, full of love and concern, reminded me of why I couldn't give up. They were my reason, my motivation. In their eyes, I saw the people I had to keep fighting for, the ones who needed me and relied on me. The love they gave me was a lifeline, a reason to push through, even when everything in me screamed to stop.

In the quiet moments, when the noise of fear and doubt started to overwhelm me, I knew that I had to dig deep. I couldn't let the exhaustion win. I couldn't let the darkness take hold of me. It was as though I was standing at the edge of a cliff, teetering between despair and hope, and I had to choose which path I would walk. I had so much to live for: the laughter of my children, the quiet moments with Howard, and the dreams I had yet to fulfill. I wasn't just fighting for my life; I was fighting for them, for all of us. I was fighting for the future we could still have together.

As I looked at the faces of the people I loved, I realized that the fight wasn't just about battling cancer but about embracing life, in all of its beauty and fragility. It was about showing up for my family, my friends, and, most importantly, myself. It was about honoring the love that surrounded me and not allowing this disease to steal my joy. I had to keep going because the life I had before was worth fighting for. The hope that still resided within me was worth fighting for.

Deep down inside, I knew I wasn't alone in this battle. I trusted in God's presence with me through every painful step, every hospital visit, and every sleepless night. I believed that God was walking beside me, carrying me when I couldn't walk on my own. And though I felt the weight of my struggle, I knew I had to want to live more than anyone else wanted me to. I had to believe in the strength and power within me, to believe that I could overcome this if I kept choosing life every day.

One of my favorite scriptures became my anchor during those tough times: "A thousand may fall at your side, ten thousand at your right hand, but it will not come near you." (Psalm 91:7). These words wrapped around me like a shield, giving me strength when I felt too weak to continue. I clung to the promise of protection, believing that even in a battle, I could be shielded by God's grace and presence. It was a reminder that no matter how hard the journey became, I wasn't walking it alone.

The support from my immediate family and my church family was also a constant source of strength. The love, prayers, and encouragement that flowed from them were a lifeline that kept me going. They stood beside me, lifted me when I couldn't do it myself, and covered me in prayer when I couldn't find the words. Knowing that I had people who cared for me and were rooting for me made all the difference. Their unwavering support reminded me that I was never truly alone, even in my darkest moments.

Howard, especially, became my rock throughout this entire journey. He treated me like a queen, showing me love and tenderness when I was at my most vulnerable. In the moments when I felt unlovable or defeated, he saw me for who I truly was: strong, worthy, and capable of overcoming this. His unwavering presence at doctor's appointments, his calmness in the face of fear, and the comfort of his hand holding mine all meant more to me than words could express. He was my constant, my support, and my partner in every sense of the word.

But it wasn't just me who was going through this battle. My family, Howard, Shatay, and Markell, went through this with me as well. They saw and felt my pain, my fear, and my uncertainty. They spent sleepless nights worrying about me and endured the emotional rollercoaster right alongside me. My fight became their fight. They walked beside me every step of the way, offering their strength when I had none of my own. Together, we fought, not just for my survival, but for the life we knew we could still have, no matter how difficult the road was.

Through all of this, I came to realize that my mental and emotional health was just as important as my physical health. The emotional toll cancer takes can be just as devastating as the physical toll. I had to nurture my mind and spirit with just as much care as I did my body. When I felt like giving up, I leaned on God's Word, my faith, my family, and the love that surrounded me. In those moments, I found the strength to keep going, one step at a time and one day at a time. I learned to focus not just on surviving, but on living, and on embracing the journey, even in its hardest moments.

The battle was not easy, nor was it quick. There were days I wanted to curl up and hide from the world. But in the depths of my exhaustion and pain, I found a well of strength I never knew I had. And every time I thought I couldn't go on, I found a reason to keep fighting: for my family, for my faith, for the love of my tribe and community, and for the hope that, no matter what, I could make it through to the other side. I believed this scripture with all that was in me: "I can do all things through Him who gives me strength" (Philippians 4:13). It reminded me that with God's strength, there is nothing too difficult to overcome.

4

. . .

RELATIONSHIPS: HOW CANCER CHANGES EVERYTHING

Cancer has a way of turning everything upside down, and the relationships that once felt stable and predictable were suddenly tested in ways I never imagined. The impact it had on my relationship with my husband, Howard, my children, Shatay and Markell, my extended family, and even my church family was profound. But through it all, we grew closer, finding new depths of trust, love, and dependence on God.

In the beginning, it was hard to communicate how I felt. It seemed like no one could truly understand the mental and emotional toll cancer had on me. The fear, the uncertainty, the frustration all felt like too much to put into words. When I couldn't express myself, Howard was there, holding me close until I felt peace or drifted to sleep. His comforting presence became my anchor on nights when I felt overwhelmed by everything. He never once hesitated, never once complained. He just held me.

Cancer doesn't just affect the person diagnosed. It ripples through the entire family. Howard not only had to stand by my side through doctor's appointments and treatments, but he also had to take on so many responsibilities around the house. Despite working a full-time job, he did most of the cooking and housework. I was no longer able to take care of those things myself, and he stepped up without question. His love and dedication during that time were nothing short of extraordinary. I'm not sure how he found the strength to do it all, but he did.

It wasn't just Howard who helped. My parents and siblings also rallied around me. They would come and stay for a week at a time, offering support, helping with the kids, and taking care of things I couldn't manage. Their presence brought a sense of comfort and normalcy, even as everything else felt chaotic. Their love was like a balm to my weary soul. I don't think they'll ever fully know just how much their support meant to me.

At the same time, I found myself leaning on relationships I never expected. Through my journey, I connected with other survivors. We shared our stories, our fears, and our victories. It was a unique bond that only someone who had walked the same path could understand. I found great strength in their courage, and I tried to be a source of strength for those struggling in the moment. There were times when I wasn't sure if I could continue, but knowing that I could lift someone else's spirits helped me keep going. It was as if we were all walking together, supporting each other through this shared experience.

Cancer had a way of changing everything, but it also deepened the relationships that mattered most. It taught us all how to lean on God more than we ever had before. It taught us how to trust one another in ways we never had before. Through it all, we grew closer and were united by love, faith, and the shared determination to face each day as a family, a community, and a support system.

Supporting Family Members Through the Journey

To the families and loved ones of those going through breast cancer, your role in this journey is incredibly important. The emotional and physical toll that cancer takes on us (the patient) is immense, and your support can make all the difference.

Here are some tips for family members on how to support your loved one during their battle with breast cancer:

1. **Be Present, Not Just Physically, but Emotionally**

   Sometimes, just being there with a listening ear can mean the world. Your loved one may not always want to talk about their diagnosis or treatment, but knowing you're there, ready to listen, will bring comfort. Let them express their feelings without judgment, and don't feel the need to always have the "right" answer.

2. **Understand the Emotional Rollercoaster**

   Cancer brings a complex mix of emotions: fear, sadness, frustration, anger, even joy and relief. It's important to acknowledge and validate these feelings, rather than try to "fix" them. Sometimes, the best you can do is offer a hug or sit in silence together.

3. **Be Patient and Flexible**

   Your loved one's needs may change daily or even hourly. Some days they may feel strong, other days they may feel exhausted or emotional. Be patient and flexible in how you support them. Ask them what they need on any given day, whether it's help with chores, assistance with medical appointments, or simply a comforting presence.

4. Take Care of Yourself, Too

Caring for a loved one with cancer can be physically and emotionally draining. You need to find moments for self-care as well. Reach out for support when you need it, whether it's through friends, family, or support groups for caregivers. By taking care of yourself, you'll be better equipped to care for your loved one.

5. Help with Practical Tasks

Cancer treatment can often leave a patient fatigued and physically drained. Offer to help with everyday tasks like cooking, cleaning, childcare, or running errands. Taking some of these tasks off their plate will allow them to focus on healing.

6. **Encourage Self-Care and Activities**

   Encourage your loved one to continue engaging in activities that bring them joy, whether it's reading, watching movies, or spending time with family. Cancer treatment can be isolating, so finding ways to keep them involved and connected with their passions is vital for their emotional health.

7. **Respect Boundaries**

   Everyone copes with cancer differently. Some people may want to talk about it openly, while others may want to keep their experience private. Respect their boundaries, and if they want to share their feelings, be ready to listen without offering unsolicited advice.

8. **Be a Source of Hope**

   Cancer patients can sometimes lose hope or feel like giving up. Your encouragement, hope, and positive energy can help lift their spirits. However, it's also important to be real and acknowledge the struggles while reminding them that they are strong and capable of getting through this.

9. **Stay Informed, But Don't Overwhelm**

While it's important to learn about breast cancer and its treatments, avoid overwhelming your loved one with too much information. Keep up-to-date on their medical journey, but always ask them if they want to talk about new treatment options or side effects. Offer your support, but let them guide the conversation.

10. **Celebrate Small Wins**

Every little victory counts. Whether it's completing a round of chemotherapy, hearing that a treatment is working, or just getting through a particularly tough day, celebrate those moments. Acknowledge the progress, no matter how small, to help boost morale and keep the focus on recovery.

5

. . .

LIFE OUTSIDE CANCER: NAVIGATING DAILY LIFE

Life, as I knew it, was no longer the same. The familiar routines, the sense of stability, and the everyday joys I had once taken for granted were replaced by a new and unfamiliar rhythm. Cancer and its treatments had a profound impact on every aspect of my daily life. I found myself in uncharted territory, struggling to adapt to this new normal. Some days, it felt like I was going through the motions: getting up, going through the day-to-day tasks, etc. On the inside, I was a storm of emotions and uncertainty. It was as if my body and mind were at odds, desperately trying to find some sense of balance amid the chaos. But somehow, despite the turmoil, I learned to adjust and adapt to the rhythm of living through cancer treatments.

During radiation, I was fortunate enough to continue working, which proved to be a blessing. My job became a lifeline, a thread of normalcy during all the change. It gave me something to focus on outside of my treatments, a reason to get out of bed and keep moving forward. I would go to work and do my best to keep up with the tasks. Even when my body was telling me it needed rest, I'd feel a sense of accomplishment. But once chemotherapy started, everything changed. I had to acknowledge that I could no longer carry on at the same pace I had been accustomed to. In the early days of chemo, I pushed myself to keep up with my routine of attending doctor's visits, running errands, and even going to church, where the support and prayers from my community provided a sense of peace and encouragement. But after the third treatment, the weight of fatigue and the toll chemo was taking on my body became undeniable. I could no longer push myself to maintain the facade of normalcy. It was time to listen to my body and take a leave from work to focus on my health and rest.

Chemotherapy was brutal. The treatments drained me in ways I could never have imagined. The first few days after each round were the hardest. The fatigue that came with each session hit me like a freight train. By the third day, I could barely lift my head off the pillow. My energy levels were non-existent, and the simplest of tasks, like taking a shower or making a meal, felt like monumental efforts. I spent most of my time at home, surrounded by the four walls that seemed to close in on me. The isolation was hard to bear at times, but I also found solace in the quiet moments of rest, knowing my body was trying to heal. Howard, my ever-supportive husband, was my rock. On the weeks between treatments, when I could muster the energy, he would take me for short drives, just for a change of scenery and a brief escape from the routine of doctor's visits and resting. The fresh air, the trees, and the sky were like a breath of life, a small reminder that there was a world beyond my struggle.

Throughout this journey, I prayed fervently. I prayed for the treatments to be effective, and for my body to endure and heal. I asked God to guide every pill I took and every treatment I underwent. I prayed for His protection over me and that the treatments and drugs would do what they were designed to do, to kill the cancer cells without causing harm to my body. I knew that as long as I kept the faith, as long as God was in the middle of it all, I could face whatever came my way. I had to trust that He was in control, even when everything else seemed out of control.

As the days turned into weeks, it sometimes felt like life was passing me by. People around me were going on with their routines surrounding work, family, school, and travel. I felt as though I was stuck in a constant cycle of treatments, fatigue, and recovery. I couldn't help but feel disconnected from the life I had known. Even so, deep down, I knew this was just a season. The treatments would eventually end, and I would regain my strength. That being said, it was so hard. Every day felt like a battle between my body's limitations and my will to continue. I had to remind myself that this was temporary, and it wasn't a reflection of who I was or what my life would become. The emotional and physical toll of the treatments was real, but so was my resolve to persevere and rise above the challenges.

Radiation became a daily routine for seven weeks. Every day, I drove to the radiology center, walked through the sterile waiting rooms, and lay on the treatment table. At first, the monotony of it all felt draining, but, with time, it became a helpful part of a ritual, a step closer to being healed. It was a reminder that I was doing everything in my power to fight this battle, no matter how tiring it was. Similarly, chemotherapy brought its own source of exhaustion. Treatments were scheduled every two or three weeks, depending on my blood counts. Each session left me feeling utterly depleted. But despite the toll it took, I held onto the belief that each treatment brought me one step closer to being cancer-free.

Once the treatments ended, a new reality set in: the follow-up appointments. I thought I would feel a sense of relief. Instead, I found myself bracing for the next round of tests and doctor's visits. The cancer may have been in remission, but it cast a lingering shadow. My doctors monitored me closely due to reoccurrences, scheduling visits every three to six months to make sure the cancer had not returned. While the worst seemed to be behind me, I was constantly reminded that the road to full recovery would be lengthy.

Those check-ups, while important for my health, became a reminder of how fragile life could be.
At the same time, they gave me peace of mind, knowing that I was being cared for. The fight was not quite over, but I had a team supporting me every step of the way.

The hardest part was learning how to live in this new reality. I had to adjust to the rhythm of life after cancer, navigating the emotional and physical changes that came with it. There were days when it felt like the weight of it all would crush me, but after looking at my children and husband, I would remember this was just a chapter in my story. It wasn't the end, but a new beginning. With each passing day, I learned to embrace the new normal, to live with purpose, and to honor the strength I had found in myself throughout this journey. Life after cancer wasn't easy, but it was still life. I was determined to live it fully, with gratitude and hope.

6

• • •

FINDING A NEW NORMAL: LIFE AFTER TREATMENT

The road to recovery was not always easy, but it was full of blessings. One of the greatest blessings was the opportunity to help others who were walking the same difficult path. I remember the feeling of being lost and uncertain when I was first diagnosed, and now I would have the chance to offer hope and support to those who needed it most. I knew that despite all I had been through, I could still be a light for others who were facing their battles with cancer.

Life after treatment required me to adjust to my "new normal." Things weren't the same, and I had to accept that. With lymphedema, I had to be very careful about lifting any significant amount of weight and any activity that could potentially worsen the condition. Managing the fluid buildup became a daily task that I couldn't ignore. Brain fog was another side effect of the treatments that I had to endure. I often felt like my mind wasn't as sharp as it once was, and simple tasks sometimes felt overwhelming. It was a frustrating reality, but as I learned to cope, over time, things started to improve.

One of the hardest parts of treatment was the inevitable hair loss. Watching my hair fall out was not just a physical loss; it felt like I was losing part of my identity as a woman. Hair, for many of us, represents beauty, femininity, and self-expression. The thought of losing it was deeply unsettling.

I reached a point where I had to **take control** of the situation. Instead of waiting for it all to fall out in clumps, I had my husband, Howard, cut it off. It wasn't an easy choice, but, in that moment, I knew I had to face reality and take charge of it. Howard, ever supportive, stood by me as I took that step. I watched as he carefully cut each section of my hair. As each lock fell away, I knew I was taking back some control in a situation where I felt so powerless. It wasn't easy, but it was empowering. I realized that even though cancer had taken away so much, it couldn't take away my strength to face this.

At first, I wasn't sure how I would feel about being completely bald. Would I feel exposed? Would people stare at me? Would I still feel beautiful? It was a challenge to embrace, but over time, I **unlocked a new level of confidence, even with the bald head**. I realized that confidence didn't come from my hair or outward appearance. It came from within. I was still me and still had so much to offer. Through this experience, I discovered that true beauty is not defined solely by what's on the outside. It's shown in how you handle life's challenges, how you treat others, and how you carry yourself with grace, no matter what you may come up against.

After I cut my hair off, I was ready to come out of the wig. It was hot and uncomfortable, and I didn't feel like me anymore. Initially, I wore the wig because I was self-conscious about my bald head. However, as more time passed, I realized it was more about the emotional comfort than the physical discomfort. The wig gave me a sense of normalcy; it was a security blanket during a time when everything felt so uncertain.

Eventually, I couldn't stand it any longer. I wanted to embrace the real me, bald head and all. It was freeing to let go of the wig and face the world just as I was. It wasn't easy at first, but I grew to love my bald head. It was a reminder of my strength, my resilience, and the battle I was fighting. Plus, it gave me a newfound sense of confidence.

Howard was especially protective of me during that time. At first, he didn't want me to show my bald head.

I think he worried about how people would react and how I would feel about it. Honestly, I didn't know what to expect either. I was unsure what people would think or say when they saw me without hair. It was a vulnerable feeling to expose this part of myself that I wasn't sure I was ready to share.

Even with my reservations, that wig was hot, itchy, and heavy. I knew I had to come out from under it for myself. In the end, the wig became a symbol of the old me, the version trying to hide from the reality of my illness. As time went on, something changed in me. I realized that my bald head was not something to hide. It was part of my journey, part of the battle I was fighting. I came to embrace it as a testimony. My hair loss wasn't a sign of weakness; it was a symbol of strength and survival. It was a reflection of the battle I had been through and the hope that I carried within me. This new revelation was one of the most empowering moments in my journey.

I also realized that many people didn't know the full extent of what I was going through. To the outside world, I probably just looked like a woman choosing to wear a wig. The truth was my bald head underneath that wig had a story, and it was finally time to tell it. I knew letting people in about my experience could be a way to witness and share that story with others.

Embracing my bald head became about more than just my appearance. It became a way to start conversations, share my testimony, and show others that no matter what life throws at us, we can still stand tall and find strength. That bald head was not just a signifier of the struggle but also of the victory and the faith that carried me through.

I have become better, not bitter. This mantra and perspective shift I adapted was one of the most important and valuable lessons learned through this journey. The challenges, the hardships, and the pain could have made me resentful. Instead, it made me more appreciative of life and all its gifts. Cancer forced me to evaluate what really mattered and what was worth holding onto. The little annoyances that once seemed so important no longer had the same power over me. I learned not to sweat the small stuff. The small arguments, trivial worries, and minor annoyances all faded away. Life can be short, and I didn't want to waste my time on things that didn't truly matter.

I also learned to **get over things quickly**. There's no time to hold grudges or stay upset over minor issues when you've been through something as significant and life changing as cancer. I learned that forgiveness was a gift I gave myself, and holding onto negativity only stole precious moments from my loved ones and me.

I began to appreciate the value of **every moment**. Life is unpredictable, and, after all the uncertainty I'd faced, I realized how precious time is. I chose to savor the little moments, show love fully, and make sure those around me knew how much they meant to me. I embraced the chance to love hard. Life is too short to do anything less.

7

. . .

THE POWER OF HOPE AND COMMUNITY

Throughout my cancer journey, I learned something crucial: **no one fights alone**. When I was first diagnosed, I had no idea how I would navigate the storm ahead. The weight of the news, the uncertainty, and the fear felt suffocating. As I moved through the process, however, I realized just how important the support of my tribe would be. I could never have made it through without the unwavering love, prayers, and encouragement from my church family, friends, and the broader community around me.

Their support lifted me on the days when I thought I couldn't keep going, reminding me that even in my weakest moments, I wasn't truly alone.

My pastors and church family were there from the very beginning. They showered me with prayers, comfort, and emotional support. They provided not only spiritual guidance but also practical help during the most challenging times. When the weight of the battle seemed insurmountable, their words of faith and encouragement carried me through some of my hardest days. I found solace in their consistent presence, in their unwavering belief that God had a plan for me, even if I couldn't see it at the time.

It was incredible to witness the power of community and how a group of people could come together and offer such tangible support. When you're facing something as isolating as cancer, it's easy to feel like you're fighting a battle alone.

Fear can make you feel so small and isolated, but having a community of people who were willing to walk beside me, pray with me, and share their own stories of hope made all the difference in the world. They reminded me, day after day, that I was not in this fight by myself.

I also found strength in giving back. I began volunteering at the local cancer center, sharing my story with others who were beginning their journeys with cancer. It wasn't easy; at times, I could barely find the energy to care for myself, let alone help someone else. However, as I spoke with newly diagnosed patients and offered words of hope and encouragement, something within me shifted. I realized that healing often comes not just through the treatment we receive but also through helping others. By sharing my story, I discovered that I wasn't just a cancer patient. I was a survivor with a story that could inspire others. Each time I offered a word of hope or gave someone the space to express her fears, I was reminded of how far I'd come. I was reminded of the strength I had within me and that I had so much more to live for. This exchange of support became an essential part of my healing process.

Being involved in a breast cancer support group was another pivotal part of my journey. There was something uniquely powerful about talking to others facing the same challenges. We didn't have to explain our fears or frustrations; they understood because they lived it. Sharing experiences and offering mutual encouragement became an invaluable part of my recovery. It wasn't just about finding practical advice or medical information; it was about sharing our collective strength and leaning on each other. There was an unspoken bond between us, one that transcended words. We were a community of survivors, and that connection became my lifeline. These groups became a safe space to express my fears, hopes, and the unique struggles I faced without judgment. In return, I received the support I desperately needed.

It was a reminder that while each of our journeys was different, we were all in it together. Together, we were stronger.

It wasn't just the support groups or the people who shared similar experiences that made a difference in my life. I chose to surround myself with people who spoke life into me. The words we hear, especially when we're going through something as life-altering as cancer, have a profound impact on our mindset. It became paramount for me to intentionally surround myself with individuals who spoke words of hope, love, inspiration, and encouragement over me. I didn't have time for negativity or people who brought fear into the equation. In the battle for my health, I needed to hear that there was light at the end of the tunnel, that I would make it through, and that I had a purpose to fulfill on the other side. Every encouraging word, every prayer, and every expression of love became a piece of armor that shielded me from despair. It became the foundation I needed to keep going.

Being in the presence of people gave me hope when it felt like I had none left. Hope became my anchor, the one thing that kept me grounded when the storms of doubt and fear threatened to consume me. It was the one constant in a world that felt turned upside down. Hope, I learned, is not just a fleeting feeling but a choice. A choice to keep moving forward, even when the path ahead seems unclear. It's the decision to believe that, despite the overwhelming challenges, better days are ahead. My community became the place where my hope was nourished and strengthened. Through the love and support of my church family, friends, and fellow survivors, I was constantly reminded that I didn't have to fight alone. Together, we were stronger. Together, we could face anything.

I will forever be grateful for the power of hope and the incredible strength of being surrounded by a loving, supportive community. It's a lesson I'll carry with me for the rest of my life: we're never alone in our struggles, and the power of hope can carry us through even the darkest of times. Through the grace of God and the love of those around me, I learned that healing isn't just about the body; it's about the spirit and the strength we draw from others as we navigate life's challenges.

There will be days when life seems to knock us flat on the ground. Having strength doesn't mean we never fall. It means we find the courage to rise again. Each time we rise, our faith grows stronger, and our hope reaches further. That's exactly what I had to do: keep rising one battle and one day at a time.

⌀

• • •

A NEW PERSPECTIVE:
CANCER'S UNEXPECTED GIFTS

I never imagined something as devastating as a breast cancer diagnosis would offer me anything I'd be grateful for. But as I went through the grueling treatments, the ups and downs, the uncertainties, and the recovery, I came to realize that, in a way, cancer gave me unexpected gifts. These gifts reshaped my life and my perspective in profound ways.

The first gift was **a deeper appreciation for life.** After facing the possibility of losing my life, I no longer took everyday moments for granted.

The simple joys like watching my children play, feeling the sun's warmth on my face, or enjoying a quiet evening with my husband became so much more meaningful. I learned to savor every second because life is fragile and precious. The things I once thought were trivial or insignificant now felt monumental. I learned to embrace the present and to never wait for the "perfect" moment to show love or take risks. I had to live life on purpose, fully, right then and there.

Another unexpected gift was **an enhanced sense of strength**. When faced with a challenge like cancer, you have no choice but to dig deep and find the strength you didn't know you had. Cancer pushed me to my limits physically, emotionally, and spiritually. Yet, each time I thought I couldn't go on, I found a new well of strength to draw from. It was a reminder that I am resilient and able to face the toughest of battles and still rise above them. This new sense of strength has stayed with me, long after the treatments ended.

Cancer also gave me **a deeper connection to my loved ones**. My relationships with my husband, children, family, and friends grew stronger. I witnessed the unwavering support of my community, the sacrifices made, and the kindness given. My husband, Howard, showed me a love that went beyond words. He cared for me in ways I didn't even know I needed. My children, though young, showed me how much joy can be found in the simple moments of life. Cancer brought us closer together in ways that words can't fully capture. We learned how to lean on each other more deeply, to love more fiercely, and to cherish every moment together.

Additionally, cancer gave me **a new perspective on my health and body**. I realized my body wasn't just a vessel to carry me through life; it was a temple that deserved care, respect, and appreciation. I started to listen to my body in ways I never had before, paying attention to its signals and needs. One of the hardest lessons I'd learned was that I don't have to be everything to everyone. It's okay to not always be available. Sometimes, the most loving thing I can do for myself and others is to say no when I need to protect my peace and focus on my own well-being.

Another priority I made was a dedication to **eat healthier and exercise regularly**. This wasn't a decision made out of fear but of love and respect for the body that had fought so hard to survive. These healthier choices have become a fundamental part of my life. The journey also prompted me to take better care of myself, something I now view as an ongoing commitment to my wellbeing.

The most significant and unexpected gift, perhaps, was how cancer **reshaped my faith**. When I was first diagnosed, I thought I had a strong faith, but cancer forced me to truly **walk out** what I said I believed. I had to put my faith into action in ways I had never imagined. It was easy to trust God when everything was going well, but when my world was turned upside down, my faith was truly tested. I had to choose daily to believe that God was with me, that I wasn't alone in this battle, and that there was a purpose in my pain.

This journey was a spiritual one just as much as it was a physical and emotional one. It was a refining process, and though it wasn't easy, I came out on the other side with a faith that was stronger, deeper, and more rooted than before. I learned to lean on God not just in the moments of crisis but also in every moment of life. Cancer forced me to trust God in ways I hadn't before, to release my need for control, and to rely on His strength instead of my own. It gave me a deeper sense of peace, knowing that my life was in His hands, no matter what.

I believed that God trusted me with this journey. In the quiet moments of reflection, I felt a deep conviction that He knew I wouldn't give up. He saw something in me, something stronger than I often saw in myself. He knew I had the strength to persevere, to face the darkest moments, and to persevere. It wasn't easy, and there were times I questioned why I had to endure this pain.

Despite my questioning, in my heart, I believed that He was guiding me through the process. I had to stay the course and endure. It wasn't a straight path, and there were times when I wanted to skip ahead to the end. I wanted to get to the healing, to the peace. I realized, though, that the process itself was where the growth happened. The struggles, the setbacks, the moments of doubt, and the breakthroughs all played a part in shaping me into who I was becoming. Healing wasn't just about the body; it was also about the spirit, the mind, and the heart.

I had to trust in His plan, even when I couldn't see the end. I had to trust that the pain would not last forever and that I would eventually get to a place of healing and restoration. Through the test, I knew that God was with me every step of the way. Even on the days when I felt like the weight of the world was on my shoulders, I clung to the belief that He was using this trial to refine me, make me stronger, and help me become the person I was meant to be.

Through it all, I knew this wasn't just about fighting cancer. It was about trusting in God's timing, in His wisdom, and in the strength He had given me to endure. He didn't promise that the journey would be easy, but He promised He would be with me through it all. This revelation gave me the courage to face each day, one step at a time.

Lastly, cancer gave me **the gift of empathy**. It opened my eyes to the struggles others face, especially those battling illness, loss, or hardship. Through my own experience, I learned how important it is to offer compassion and understanding to others. I could connect with people on a deeper level. These connections were made not just as a survivor but as someone who truly understood pain, fear, hope, and resilience. This gift of empathy has allowed me to be a better friend, mother, and advocate for those who are going through trials.

Cancer brought so much pain and fear into my life, but it also brought with it these unexpected gifts. Because of them, I have changed in ways I could have never expected. **A deeper appreciation for life, the strength I didn't know I had, closer connections to my loved ones, a renewed sense of health and self-care, a reshaped faith, and greater empathy for others**: these are the gifts I now carry with me. And for that, I am deeply grateful.

CONCLUSION

. . .

THE ROAD AHEAD: CONTINUING THE JOURNEY

Today, I stand at a place in my life I never imagined I would reach. After everything I've gone through, I find myself in a better and brighter place than ever before. My health has greatly improved, and, while I continue to stay under the care of my physicians, there's something deeper that I rely on every day: I am in God's care, and I trust that His hands are holding me. My life has a purpose! I have found peace in knowing that despite the battles I faced, I am exactly where I am meant to be.

THE STRENGTH THAT RISES FROM WITHIN

As I stand on the other side of this journey, I realize that what began as a battle for survival became so much more. It was never just about fighting cancer, it was about rediscovering the strength I forgot I had, the love that surrounded me, and the unshakable will to keep moving forward, no matter how uncertain the path may have seemed.

I had a choice to either grow bitter or grow better. Bitterness would have chained me to my pain, but hope invited me to heal. Choosing hope was the moment I found the strength within me beginning to rise. That choice changed everything for me.

It's undeniable that cancer changed me, but it didn't define me. I may have faced moments of fear, uncertainty, and pain, but I also found resilience in the darkest times. I learned to let go of things that didn't matter and embrace the things that truly did. The people I love, the simple pleasures of life, and the beauty of each day were all things I might have taken for granted before, but now I see them and their value with clear eyes.

It's deeply concerning that despite advances in treatment and awareness, an alarming number of women still die from breast cancer each year.

It remains one of the leading causes of cancer-related deaths in women worldwide, with many of these deaths being preventable with early detection. One of the most significant reasons for this disparity is that many women in our community aren't getting regular screenings or are unaware of how critical early detection is. To change this grim reality, we must break the silence and educate ourselves. Early detection is key to survival. We cannot wait. It must become a routine part of our lives to perform regular breast self-exams, schedule mammograms, get clinical breast exams, and learn to listen to our bodies. By being proactive and informed, we empower ourselves to take control of our health. Knowing our bodies and being aware of any changes gives us the best chance to detect potential issues ahead of time.

Understanding our family history and risk factors is equally important, as it can guide us in making informed decisions about screenings and preventative care.

Taking these steps isn't just about being healthy; it's about protecting our lives and the lives of those we love. We must become advocates for our health. If something looks or feels off, we cannot ignore it. If something looks different, we must get it checked out. Early detection of breast cancer is a crucial factor in improving outcomes, survival rates, and overall quality of life. The sooner you catch it, the sooner you can begin treatment. During the earliest stages, it is often more treatable, less likely to spread, and gives patients a higher chance of a full recovery. Early detection isn't just a medical term; it's a lifesaver.

I know that the medical community is working tirelessly in the search for a cure, but we cannot rely on others to fix everything. We have to take responsibility for our health. I am incredibly grateful for the doctors and medical professionals who guided me along my journey, but I also recognize that God is the ultimate healer and was in the midst of it all. I never lost faith that He was with me, and it's that faith that carried me through the darkest moments. His presence was my strength when I thought I had none left. It's still that same faith that continues to guide me as I walk through the remainder of my life.

In the years since my diagnosis, I am definitely not the same person I was before. I am stronger, more resilient, and more grateful than I could have ever imagined. I've learned that life's challenges don't break us. They shape us. I can say with full confidence that I am better for this experience and not bitter. After 23 years, I may have some limitations, but I have my life. I am healthy. I am whole. I am an overcomer. I am a champion, a testament to the power of resilience, faith, and hope.

This journey taught me that healing comes in more than just the physical form. It's emotional, mental, and spiritual. I've learned to be kinder to myself, to appreciate my body for what it has endured, and to embrace the vulnerability that comes with survival. Most importantly, perhaps, I've learned that it's okay not to have all the answers. Life is uncertain, and while the future may be unpredictable, it's also a place full of infinite possibilities.

As I continue my journey, I'm reminded that the road ahead won't always be easy, but I have the tools I need to navigate it. I have my faith, my strength, my community, and my purpose. I want to be a voice for others who are facing the same fight, share the lessons I've learned, and encourage others not to give up. There is life after cancer. There is joy, there is peace, and there is always hope.

To anyone reading this, know that you are not alone. No matter what your circumstances may be, there is always a way forward. Hold on to hope. Seek out support. Trust in the journey. Know that you are stronger than you think. The road ahead may have its challenges, but, with each step, we grow stronger. I'm walking this road, I'm not turning back, and neither should you.

No matter what you are facing right now, you are not powerless. God has already placed a strength within you that is greater than any storm around you. You may feel weak, but that strength is rising even now. You can rise. You can overcome.

Keep fighting, keep hoping, and keep believing. The best is yet to come!

Let's continue to raise our voices, take control of our health, and never stop believing in the power of hope and resilience. Early detection of breast cancer is so crucial, giving patients a much higher chance of successful treatment and full recovery. Together, we can make a difference.

A MESSAGE TO WOMEN FACING THEIR BREAST CANCER JOURNEY

To all the women dealing with breast cancer, I want you to know that you are not alone. The road ahead may seem overwhelming, and, at times, it may feel like more than you can bear. I promise you are stronger than you think. You have the power within you to face this challenge with courage and hope for a brighter future.

I know the uncertainty of treatments, the physical changes, and the emotional toll can be exhausting. Remember, every step you take, big or small, is a step toward healing. Lean into the support of those around you: your family, your friends, and your community. Don't be afraid to reach out for help, share your fears, and embrace the love and prayers that surround you.

This journey will not define you; it will refine you. You are more than your diagnosis. You are a warrior, a survivor, and a testament to strength. There will be difficult days, but there will also be victories, moments of peace, and even joy. Trust in yourself, and know that with each day, you are one step closer to recovery.

Most importantly, never lose hope. Your faith, your spirit, and your courage are powerful tools that will carry you through. You will overcome. And when you do, you'll emerge with a deeper understanding of your strength and resilience.

You are not alone, and you are loved. Keep fighting, keep believing, and keep going. You've got this.

THE STRENGTH THAT RISES FROM WITHIN

Here are some scriptures that kept me encouraged and uplifted during my journey:

1. Jeremiah 30:17 (NIV)
" 'But I will restore you to health and heal your wounds,' declares the Lord."
- This verse is a reminder that God is the ultimate healer. He promises to restore your health and bring healing.

2. Isaiah 41:10 (NIV)
"So do not fear, for I am with you; do not be dismayed, for I am your God. I will strengthen you and help you; I will uphold you with my righteous right hand."
- Even in moments of fear and uncertainty, God promises His constant presence and support, offering the strength to keep going.

3. Psalm 34:17-18 (NIV)
"The righteous cry out, and the Lord hears them; he delivers them from all their troubles. The Lord is close to the brokenhearted and saves those who are crushed in spirit."
- In times of emotional and physical struggle, God is near to you, offering comfort, peace, and deliverance

4. Romans 8:28 (NIV)
"And we know that in all things God works for the good of those who love him, who have been called according to his purpose."
- Even in difficult times, trust that God is at work behind the scenes, turning struggles into something good.

5. Psalm 147:3 (NIV)
"He heals the brokenhearted and binds up their wounds."
- God is a healer of both the physical body and the emotional heart, offering restoration and comfort.

THE STRENGTH THAT RISES FROM WITHIN

6. Isaiah 53:5 (NIV)
"But he was pierced for our transgressions, he was crushed for our iniquities; the punishment that brought us peace was on him, and by his wounds we are healed."
- This verse reminds us of the healing that came through Christ's sacrifice, bringing both physical and spiritual healing.

7. 2 Corinthians 12:9 (NIV)
"But he said to me, 'My grace is sufficient for you, for my power is made perfect in weakness.' " Therefore I will boast all the more gladly of my weaknesses, so that the power of Christ may rest upon me."
- In times of weakness, God's grace is more than enough. It's in our weakest moments that His power is revealed.

8. Philippians 4:13 (NIV)
"I can do all this through Him who gives me strength."
- Remember, with God's strength, there is nothing too difficult to overcome.

9. Matthew 11:28-30 (NIV)
"Come to me, all you who are weary and burdened, and I will give you rest. Take my yoke upon you and learn from me, for I am gentle and humble in heart, and you will find rest for your souls. For my yoke is easy and my burden is light."
- When the weight of the journey feels overwhelming, Jesus invites you to rest in Him and trust His gentle and loving care.

10. Psalm 103:2-4 (NIV)
"Praise the Lord, my soul, and forget not all his benefits—who forgives all your sins and heals all your diseases, who redeems your life from the pit and crowns you with love and compassion."
- This scripture is a reminder that God is the healer of all things, including physical illness, and He has the power to redeem and restore.

11. Proverbs 3:5-6 (NIV)
"Trust in the Lord with all your heart and lean not on your own understanding; in all your ways submit to him, and he will make your paths straight."
- Even when things seem uncertain or overwhelming, trusting in God's plan will bring clarity and peace.

12. Romans 15:13 (NIV)
"May the God of hope fill you with all joy and peace as you trust in him, so that you may overflow with hope by the power of the Holy Spirit.
- No matter the circumstances, God fills us with joy, peace, and hope through His Spirit.

13. Jeremiah 29:11 (NIV)
"For I know the plans I have for you," declares the Lord, "plans to prosper you and not to harm you, plans to give you a hope and a future."
- Even in the face of illness, God has good plans for your life. Trust in His hope and future for you.

14. Mark 5:34 (NIV)
"He said to her, 'Daughter, your faith has healed you. Go in peace and be freed from your suffering.'"
- This is a reminder of how powerful faith is. Trusting in God's healing can bring peace and freedom from suffering.

15. Psalm 91:7 (NIV)
"A thousand may fall at your side, ten thousand at your right hand, but it will not come near you."
- This verse is a powerful reminder of God's divine protection. Even in the face of adversity and danger, God promises to keep you safe and shielded from harm. Trust that His protection surrounds you as you walk through life's challenges.

<u>NOTES</u>:

<u>NOTES</u>:

www.ingramcontent.com/pod-product-compliance
Lightning Source LLC
Chambersburg PA
CBHW061704120626
46550CB00003B/1075